M
23.93

MCR

JUL 09 2004

W9-AOM-680
3 1192 01250 9756

x553.24 Parke.S

Parker, Steve.

Coal /

c2004.

MCR

JUL 09 2004

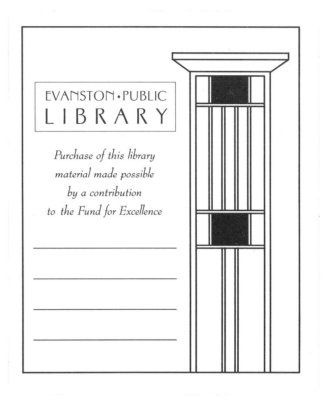

EVANSTON · PUBLIC
LIBRARY

*Purchase of this library
material made possible
by a contribution
to the Fund for Excellence*

_____

_____

_____

_____

SCIENCE FILES

energy

COAL

EVANSTON PUBLIC LIBRARY
CHILDREN'S DEPARTMENT
1703 ORRINGTON AVENUE
EVANSTON, ILLINOIS 60201

Please visit our web site at: www.garethstevens.com
For a free color catalog describing Gareth Stevens Publishing's
list of high-quality books and multimedia programs,
call 1-800-542-2595 (USA) or 1-800-387-3178 (Canada).
Gareth Stevens Publishing's fax: (414) 332-3567.

Library of Congress Cataloging-in-Publication Data

Parker, Steve.
    Coal / by Steve Parker.
        p. cm. — (Science files. Energy)
    Includes bibliographical references and index.
    ISBN 0-8368-4029-1 (lib. bdg.)
    Contents: The coal age — Coal formation — Coal deposits — Coal mines — Coal miners —
Mining coal — Mining surface coal — Transporting coal — Coal for power — Coal use in industry —
Coal products — Coal pollution — Future coal energy.
    1. Coal—Juvenile literature. [1. Coal.] I. Title.
TN801.P37   2004
553.2'4—dc22   2003060565

This North American edition first published in 2004 by
Gareth Stevens Publishing
A World Almanac Education Group Company
330 West Olive Street, Suite 100
Milwaukee, WI 53212 USA

Original edition © 2002 by David West Children's Books. First published in Great Britain
in 2002 by Heinemann Library, Halley Court, Jordan Hill, Oxford OX2 8EJ, a division
of Reed Educational and Professional Publishing Limited. This U.S. edition © 2004 by
Gareth Stevens, Inc. Additional end matter © 2004 by Gareth Stevens, Inc.

David West Editor: James Pickering
Picture Research: Carrie Haines, Carlotta Cooper
Gareth Stevens Editor: Carol Ryback
Gareth Stevens Designers: Kami Koenig, Melissa Valuch
Cover Design: Melissa Valuch

Photo Credits:
Abbreviations: (t) top, (m) middle, (b) bottom, (l) left, (r) right

CORBIS: Cover, 3, 4–5 (both), 7(r), 10(bl), 10–11(b), 11(bl), 13(b), 16–17(t), 17(m), 20(bl), 20–21,
21(tr), 22 (both), 23(bl), 23(br), 24(br), 27(bl), 28(bl), 29(tr).
Dover Books: 17(br).
Katz/FSP: 14 (both).
Mary Evans Picture Library: 6(bl).
Robert Harding Picture Library: 24–25; Gavin Hellier 6–7; H. P. Merten 8(tr); Tony Waltham 8(b),
19(tr); Carolina Biological Supp/Phototake NYC 9(mr); David Hughes 9(bm); G. & P. Corrigan
13(mr); Walter Rawlings 18(bl); Robert Francis 18–19(t); Tony Gervuis 24(bl); Tomlinson 29(tl).
Sasol Limited: 27(br).
Spectrum Colour Library: 6(r), 13(tl).
Still Pictures: Mark Edwards 5(br); Peter Frischmuth 14–15, 15(bl), 16–17(b); F. & A. Mitchler 15(br);
Thomas Raupach 19(br), 26(mr); Shehzad Nooran 21(tl); A. Maclean — Peter Arnold Inc. 21(ml);
Sabine Vielmo 25(tr).
University of Southampton: 30(mr).

All rights reserved to Gareth Stevens, Inc. No part of this book may be reproduced, stored in a
retrieval system, or transmitted in any form or by any means, electronic, mechanical, photocopying,
recording, or otherwise, without the prior written permission of the publisher except for the inclusion
of brief quotations in an acknowledged review.

Printed in the United States of America

1 2 3 4 5 6 7 8 9 08 07 06 05 04

SCIENCE FILES

energy

COAL

Steve Parker

Gareth Stevens Publishing
A WORLD ALMANAC EDUCATION GROUP COMPANY

CONTENTS

Coal can be burned for power or used as a raw material for a huge range of products — from powerful chemicals to gentle soaps.

Tall buildings (inset) house pulleys that lift coal from deep below the surface and onto sloping conveyor belts.

INTRODUCTION

Few rocks are as useful as coal — a hard, black substance valued worldwide as a source of heat energy. We burn coal in power plants, factory furnaces, railroad steam locomotives, and in stoves or fireplaces in our homes. Workers often risk their lives deep underground while mining coal. Power from burning coal drives many heavy industries. Coal also causes pollution. Like all fossil fuels, the world's coal supplies cannot last forever.

Below: Hundreds of tons of coal wait in railroad cars for their journey to a coal-fired electric-power plant (inset). The plant will burn all that coal in only a few days.

THE COAL AGE

Pick up a lump of coal and you are touching a long-gone time, even before dinosaurs roamed Earth. Most coal formed hundreds of millions of years ago, mainly during the Carboniferous Period — the "Age of Coal Formation."

WARM AND WET

During Carboniferous times, 360–286 million years ago, the world was warm and damp, much like a tropical rain forest today. Giant ferns, horsetails, and other ancient plants grew in vast, steamy swamps, marshes, and bogs, well before any dinosaurs roamed Earth. Newt-like amphibians as big as crocodiles, crow-sized dragonflies, and other prehistoric animals lived in the coal swamps. Lush green plants lived, died, piled up in the warm shallow water, and gradually turned to coal (see page 8).

Sometimes, lumps of coal contain the fossilized shapes of ferns and insects.

There were no flowers, grasses, or broadleaved trees in the Carboniferous Period. The main big plants were ferns, tree ferns, horsetails, conifers, and club mosses.

An early stage in coal formation, peat can be burned as a home heating fuel. Peat also helps crops grow, but it is in short supply.

MORE AGES OF COAL

Coal has slowly formed whenever warm, wet conditions existed in Earth's geologic history. Other main coal-forest periods include the Permian, 286–250 million years ago; Triassic, 250–206 million years ago; Jurassic, 206–144 million years ago; Cretaceous, 144–65 million years ago; and Tertiary, 65–2 million years ago. Dinosaurs lived during the middle three of these periods. More than half of today's coal is from the Carboniferous Period.

Coal for the FUTURE?

Warm, damp conditions exist in certain regions today and encourage the growth of swampy forests with moss-draped trees and creeping vines. Plant life takes millions of years to turn into coal — and then only under just the right set of temperatures and pressures.

A temperate rain forest in Washington state

COAL FORMATION

Coal formation is a continuous process. Not all coal forms in exactly the same way or with the same properties. Coal is found in a range of colors and hardnesses that release varying amounts of heat energy when burned for fuel.

RECIPE FOR COAL

Coal needs four conditions to form: plants, temperature, pressure, and plenty of time. In ancient coal forests, plants did not rot away or get eaten. They died and lay in shallow water, which slowed the decay process. Gradually, the layers of dead plants deepened ...

Lignite (brown coal) is mined near Cologne, Germany. Lignite is the softest type of coal and burns slowly with a yellow, smoky flame. It is not often used inside homes.

Coal usually forms in layers or seams pressed between other kinds of rock. Earthquakes and other fault movements may tilt coal seams into sloping — or even upright — layers.

TYPES OF COAL

Geologists classify coal as rock, fossil, or mineral. Over time, huge masses of plants slowly decay and are buried, pressed, and squashed. New layers of plant material and rock bury the older plant layers deeper, pushing them closer to the heat from Earth's hot core. Coal becomes harder, darker, and a more efficient source of fuel the deeper it is found.

Living forest
Plants thrived in warm dampness, died, and piled up in deep layers.

Peat
Submerged plants partly rot into a moist, fibrous, spongy mass.

Lignite coal
This soft coal is dry and woody, with pieces of the original plants visible.

Bituminous coal
Bituminous coal is most common, fairly hard, and its layers have a sheen.

Anthracite coal
Very hard, black, and glossy, this coal burns hottest and with the least smoke or soot.

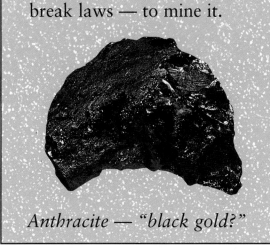

Dangerous STUFF

Anthracite is the purest form of coal. Lump for lump, this hard, black coal contains the greatest amount of stored energy, which makes it the world's most valuable coal. Anthracite occurs at great depths. Coal miners may risk their lives — and sometimes break laws — to mine it.

Anthracite — "black gold?"

ENERGY CONTENT

Heat energy is measured in kilojoules per gram (kJ/g). Lignite coal contains up to 15 kJ/g (about the same as meat), bituminous coal has 20–35 kJ/g, and anthracite coal usually has more than 30 kJ/g.

Bituminous coal is often used to heat houses.

COAL DEPOSITS

Coal is found on all of Earth's continents, including Antarctica. More than half the world's countries have some coal supplies. The coal varies greatly in quantity and quality, and in the difficulty of mining and transporting it for processing or burning.

FOSSIL FUEL

Coal is a fossil fuel — it was formed over time from once-living organisms. Earth has about one trillion tons of known coal supplies. Rock specialists called geologists and land surveyors continually search for more.

NORTH AMERICA

SOUTH AMERICA

◤ Coal-mining areas

A surveyor measures angles between hills and valleys in an area where deposits of coal might be found.

WORLD COAL SUPPLIES

Supplies of coal are widely spread throughout the world, sometimes in very small amounts. Coal also forms in remote locations or deep under Earth's surface, making it costly to mine. More than half of all known coal supplies are found in Russia, the United States, and China — countries that use the most coal. Geologists in South America, Africa, and Australia are currently looking for new coal reserves.

EUROPE

RUSSIA

AFRICA

SOUTHEAST
ASIA

AUSTRALIA

Green **ISSUES**

Coal is big business, so mining companies are constantly searching for new supplies. Mining coal can scar the land and harm wildlife. Residents, governments, and mining companies often disagree about exploring natural wilderness areas such as in Alaska and Antarctica.

HOW MUCH COAL IS LEFT?

At the present rate of use, our coal supplies should last about two hundred years — or roughly twice as long as the other two main fossil fuels:petroleum (oil) and natural gas. Geologists also expect to find as-yet-undiscovered coal deposits. Improved mining methods will also increase coal supplies for burning.

Is nature under threat?

Geologists use a test-drilling rig to remove a rod-like core of rock and examine it for coal.

COAL MINES

Coal seams are found — from Earth's surface to miles (kilometers) below ground. Over the ages, massive land movements rearrange these rock layers. When enough good-quality coal is discovered in an area, miners remove it.

Green ISSUES

Many abandoned coal mines gradually filled with water, or soil and rocks, or collapsed into shafts and chambers below. This surface sinking — called subsidence — forms depressions, or holes.

THE COAL MINE

Inside a coal mine, special machines cut coal chunks from the coal face (see page 16). Roof supports keep the mine ceiling from collapsing. Conveyor belts carry the coal and dump it in a "skip" for measuring. Cables in the winding house raise the skip up the mine shaft, empty it, and send it back for another load. A surface conveyor moves the coal to railroad cars.

Coal train
Loading tower
Winding house
Surface conveyor
Washing and sorting

Coal face
Coal cutter
Roof supports
Conveyor
Storage bunker

Mine shaft
Coal skip

12

An abandoned mine might cave in or collapse at any time, causing subsidence.

NON-STOP MINING

An automated, modern coal mine runs non-stop. Cut coal moves up conveyor belts to skips (temporary holding containers) that are then hauled up concrete shafts. Surface conveyors carry the coal to towers for washing, sorting, and grading. Afterward, the coal is loaded into railroad cars for transport.

Coal mines run twenty-four hours a day. Large pulleys inside tall winding houses hold the cables for the coal skips and workers' elevators. Lighted, sloping conveyors move coal to washing and sorting machines.

Not all coal mining operations are as automated as those in the West.

COAL MINERS

Early miners chipped coal using pickaxes. Then they hauled the coal out in bags. While such back-breaking work has nearly disappeared from modern-day coal mines, a miner's job is still hard, tiring, uncomfortable, and often dangerous. Despite enormous safety precautions, accidents still occur.

Miners descend to their work site in cage-like elevators.

HOT AND DUSTY

Some mines are about 1 mile (1,500 meters) deep. At these depths, the rock walls are very warm. The air is filtered and freshened — but still hot and humid. Mining machines are noisy, the lights glare, and black coal dust covers everything.

All miners wear a hard-hat and light, in case the general light system fails. An unlit mine is totally black.

As a mine expands, workers build new conveyors and lay rails in the tunnels and chambers where coal was once mined.

In large mines, small underground trains ferry workers long distances from the mine shaft to the coal face work site.

ALL ELECTRIC

Electricity powers the machines and lights in a mine. Gasoline or diesel engines would give off deadly fumes and use valuable oxygen that miners need to breathe. Air is filtered to remove poisonous or explosive gases that seep naturally from certain rocks. In many mines, workers fight an endless battle to pump out water that trickles in from all around.

Health RISKS

Miners should protect their lungs from coal dust by wearing masks or respirators with filters. Inhaled coal dust particles clog airways and lungs and cause wheezing, coughing, shortness of breath, and other chest illnesses with the general name of "miner's lung." Sometimes, the dust buildup in the miners' body tissue triggers different forms of cancers.

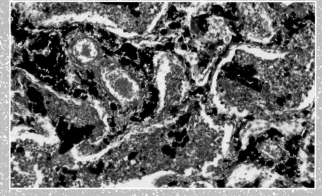

A microscope slide shows how coal dust builds up in a miner's lung.

MINING COAL

Geologists consider coal a "soft" rock — but it is a rock nonetheless, and is very hard to the touch. Large mines may remove a million tons (tonnes) of coal from the ground yearly.

SEAMS AND SHEARERS

Layers, or seams, of coal are usually discovered using hand-controlled cutters, hydraulic hammers, or even explosives. A "shearer" machine then mines that length of seam by moving along and cutting off lumps of coal as it goes. This process is called longwall mining.

THE LONGWALL

Longwall mining uses a toothed wheel called a shearer, or cutter, pressed against the coal seam. A chain pulls the slowly moving wheel along. The teeth chop away at the "long wall" of coal, which falls onto the conveyor.

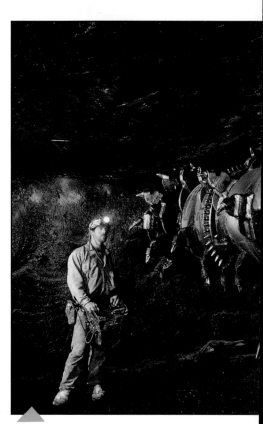

Cutters act like huge drills that bore a hole in the coal face, or they "scratch and bite" the exposed surface.

Very hard metal or tiny diamonds cover the tips of a shearer's teeth, or blades.

Rock layers

Coal seam

Guide chain pulls shearer along.

Shearer

Coal

Coal guide

Hydraulic jacks support the mine's roof and keeps pace with the shearer.

Conveyor

PILLAR-AND-ROOM

Coal removal leaves behind empty space, or "room." The pillar-and-room system leaves columns of coal holding up the rock layer above, saving the cost of roof supports. Miners cut the pillars as they work their way back out.

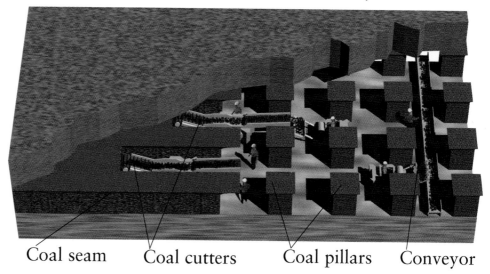

Coal seam   Coal cutters   Coal pillars   Conveyor

Holes drilled into the seam hold sticks of explosive. Loud whistles warn miners to clear the area before the upcoming blast helps loosen the coal.

MORE MINING METHODS

The longwall shearer breaks up the coal and loads it onto a conveyor or into trucks. In some mines, the seams are too short or curved for big machinery. Miners must hand-cut into the coal seams using jack-hammers or undercutters (similar to huge chainsaws) — or use explosives to blast off lumps of rock.

Old-time MINES

One hundred years ago, coal mining was an extremely risky business. Workers used picks and shovels, and wooden pit props held up the roof. The air was foul, and open candle flames often caused mine explosions.

A 19th-century coal mine

19

MINING SURFACE COAL

More than half of all coal mines are near the surface. These open-pit, or "strip" mines rely on giant diggers and excavators — machines that are often bigger than houses.

STRIP MINING

Workers commonly remove coal from strip mines in a ribbon-like pattern. They prepare each strip by scraping off the "overburden," thin layers of overlying rock and topsoil.

The removed soil is stockpiled for later replacement over the mined area. Huge diggers then move in, and a long, extended conveyor belt or trucks carry away the coal.

Sometimes a mine is so huge and in such a remote location that it has its own power plant.

STRIP MINE

The swing-arm crane, or "cutter," removes a section of coal and then moves forward to repeat the process. As the coal is mined out, rock overburden and topsoil from the areas already mined become fill that helps restore the land to its former condition.

An excavating crane scrapes away topsoil and can scoop out softer seams of coal.

Rock layer from strip being mined is put on previous strip.

Original topsoil is replaced.

Crops grow on reclaimed land.

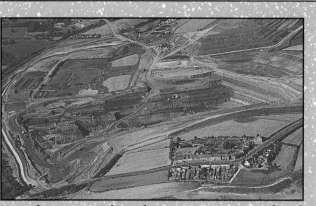

Green
ISSUES

Gaping holes from early strip mines (from about 1910) left unsightly scars on a ruined landscape. Today, strip-mined areas must be reclaimed or restored to a suitable condition. A former strip mine might become a farm, a golf course, or a sanitary landfill. The area could also be flooded to form an artificial lake.

Earth's wounds take centuries to "heal."

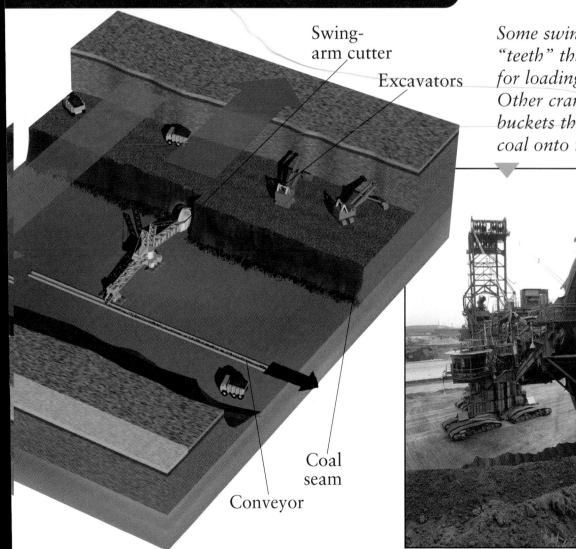

Swing-arm cutter

Excavators

Some swing-arm cutters have "teeth" that crumble the coal for loading onto the conveyor. Other cranes have a series of buckets that lift and load the coal onto the conveyor.

Coal seam

Conveyor

TRANSPORTING COAL

Coal is often mined hundreds of miles (kilometers) away from where it is used. Long trains or huge barges transport massive amounts of coal to factories and cities that burn coal for power.

COAL INFLUENCED HISTORY

Over the past few centuries, as wood supplies became scarce, industrial centers and large cities sprang up in areas near coal mines. Now that many of those early coal mines have run out, coal is shipped in from far away.

Green ISSUES

Coal mines produce enormous piles of waste, called slag. Scavengers sometimes climb the slippery, dangerous piles of slag, searching for spare lumps of coal to burn.

One of the most energy-efficient ways to move coal is by rail. Coal trains can stretch nearly 3 miles (5 km) as they pull up to 135 boxcars — each capable of holding up to 110 tons of coal.

Cargo ships and barges moor alongside electric power plants to unload their coal. Power plants burn coal to fire furnaces that turn water into steam. In turn, the steam powers turbines that produce electricity.

Children scavenge for coal.

▲ *Coal stockpiles are burned at rates that meet demand.*

EFFICIENT COAL TRANSPORT

Coal is one of the bulkiest, heaviest cargos that must be transported vast distances. Moving it by airplane or truck would cost far more than the coal itself is worth. Trains, ships, and barges provide the necessary capacity for moving hundreds of thousands of tons (tonnes) of coal in the most efficient manner possible.

TRANSOCEANIC SHIPMENTS

International, transoceanic shipping routes ferry millions of tons (tonnes) of coal to industrial regions around the world. For example, new industries in Southeast Asia — an area with few mines — get their coal from Australia.

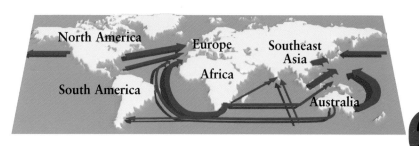

COAL FOR POWER

Coal is a form of stored chemical energy that releases its power as heat as it burns. The energy from half of the coal burned every day helps electric power plants supply about one-third of the world's electricity.

HOW GENERATORS WORK

Pressurized steam blasts against turbine blades and spins a shaft that is connected to a rotating magnet, called a rotor. As the rotor spins inside the stator, which contains loops of coiled copper wire, it produces an electromagnetic field — electricity — that flows through the wires, out of the power plant, and into your home.

COAL-FIRED POWER PLANTS

Coal burns better and hotter after it is pulverized into a powder. Coal powder is mixed with preheated fresh air and blown into a boiler. Water flowing through pipes above the boiler changes into superheated steam — which spins the turbine blades. Smokestack "scrubbers" clean dirt and chemicals from the waste gases.

1 Coal is cleaned and scrubbed.

Main boiler

Air intake

2 Hot waste gases warm incoming air.

Smoke-stack

Coal ramp

Coal hopper

3 Coal is powdered and mixed with hot air.

4 Powdered coal and hot air mixture is blown into the boiler.

5 Water in pipes is heated to high-pressure steam.

6 Steam spins turbines to power the generator.

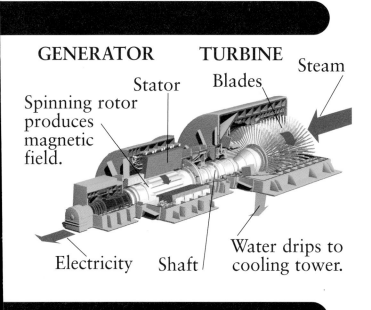

GENERATOR   **TURBINE**

Stator   Blades   Steam

Spinning rotor produces magnetic field.

Electricity   Shaft   Water drips to cooling tower.

IMPROVED ENERGY EFFICIENCY

Even in power plants that use the latest equipment, less than half the energy stored inside coal actually gets converted into electrical power. Scientists and engineers constantly search for ways to improve the efficiency of burning coal while reducing the amount of pollution created. Coal is the dirtiest fuel used in power-generating plants (see page 28).

Some cooling towers have separate water pipes that collect "spare" heat, which warms nearby buildings.

Cooling tower

7 Excess steam travels to tower.

8 Cooled water returns to main boiler.

Green **ISSUES**

Although exhaust vapors and fumes released from the smokestacks of most coal-burning power plants are cleaner than ever before, they still contain trace amounts of harmful chemicals, gases, and solid matter that build up in the environment.

Special filters "scrub" waste from fumes.

COAL USE IN INDUSTRY

Coal powers about twenty-five percent of the industries around the world. Heat from burning coal helps form iron, steel, glass, cement, plastics, rubber, pottery, chemicals, and baked goods.

THE HEAT IS ON

Coal is not a pure substance. When heated to extreme temperatures in a closed container with no air, coal separates into gases, such as coal gas and ammonia, and solids, such as coal tar and coke.

A coke furnace turns solid ore to liquid metal at about 2,900 degrees Fahrenheit (1,600 degrees Celsius).

Coal fires the boilers of steam locomotives — which are still widely used in some countries.

Smoke, soot, and fumes from coal-fired furnaces and boilers fill the skies over many industrial areas.

PROCESSING COAL

Some industries cannot use coal in its orginal form and must change it before use. Coal heated to 2,200° F (1,200 ° C) without air produces coke, while coal slow-fired in little air produces charcoal; both burn at very high temperatures. Coke fires blast furnaces that make iron and steel. Charcoal cooks food.

Green ISSUES

"Greenhouse gases" trapped in Earth's atmosphere may cause an increase in average annual temperatures — "global warming" and climate change (see page 28). Burning of a fossil fuel such as coal produces carbon dioxide (CO_2) gas, one of the harmful gases. The use of alternative energy sources could slow global warming.

STOP CO₂

FLUIDIZED BED

In fluidized bed combustion, ground-up coal and limestone burn in a very hot furnace of sand, which "boils" like a liquid. Steam powers one turbine and exhaust gases drive another, so the process produces less pollution overall.

Gases to turbine

Steam to turbine

Floating bed of fluid sand

Coal and limestone

Water

Air

25

COAL PRODUCTS

Not all coal is burned for heat energy. Some is treated by a process called gasification that produces various gases used in three main ways: to use as a raw material for industry, to burn for heat, or to power turbines.

COAL OILS AND TARS

Gasifying coal, and heating it to make coke, produces "leftovers" such as thick, gooey tars. Gases from gasification can also be cooled and turned into coal tars, oils, and similar liquids with many uses. These leftovers are processed into fertilizers for crops, cleaning solvents, preservatives like creosote and pitch, chemicals for industry, colored dyes, and even soap!

Gases and vapors given off by coke plants are cooled to form various oils, liquids, and tars, called fractions.

Green **issues**

Like any heavy industry, processing coal results in byproducts and wastes. Coal slurry may escape into waterways and damage wildlife. Certain coal tar products and solvents may cause harmful health effects, such as cancer, and must be used with great care.

A "black tide" of coal slurry

Coal-tar soap has a unique aroma and a reputation for getting skin and hair very clean. A distinctive smell also comes from mothballs, which contain the substance naphthalene — another of coal's many chemical products.

COAL GASIFIER

In a gasifier, coal is brought into contact with steam and oxygen gas. The coal does not actually burn or combust, but at such a high temperature and pressure, its chemical substances break apart or "crack" into smaller, lighter substances, especially gas fuels — which are bottled or stored and burned later. The heat energy in the gasifier boils water into steam that powers turbines and generates electricity in the usual way.

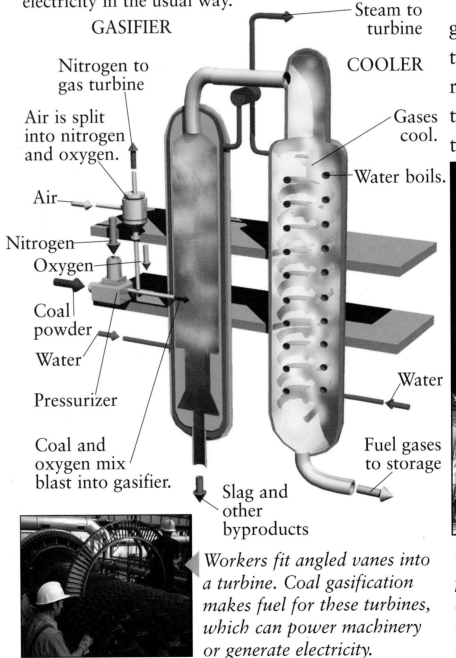

GASIFIER

Steam to turbine

Nitrogen to gas turbine

COOLER

Air is split into nitrogen and oxygen.

Gases cool.

Air

Water boils.

Nitrogen

Oxygen

Coal powder

Water

Pressurizer

Water

Coal and oxygen mix blast into gasifier.

Fuel gases to storage

Slag and other byproducts

Workers fit angled vanes into a turbine. Coal gasification makes fuel for these turbines, which can power machinery or generate electricity.

BETTER RESULTS

Overall, gasifying coal to make fuel gases that are then burned results in less pollution than burning the coal itself. Also, the gasifying process yields useful raw materials. In new "hybrid" systems, coal is first gasified and the leftovers are then burned. This process releases more than half of the heat energy locked up in the coal.

This South African chemical factory produces AO-octene partly from coal. AO-octene is used to produce thin, transparent, and clingy plastic wrapping sheets.

COAL POLLUTION

In past centuries, big cities such as London, England, choked with smoke and fumes from coal-fired industries, power plants, and millions of home furnaces. People died from lung diseases. New laws have helped clean the air, but coal still causes much pollution.

🌍 *Green* **ISSUES**

Coal burning, vehicle exhaust, and chemical factories are only a few of the sources of air pollution. Researchers believe that air pollutants may contribute to the steep rise in asthma and other health problems.

THE GREENHOUSE EFFECT

As our world becomes more industrialized and burns more coal and other fossil fuels, carbon dioxide levels in the atmosphere will rise. Earth's atmosphere acts like the glass in a greenhouse, trapping the Sun's heat, rather than letting it escape back into space. World temperatures rise.

Energy is reflected back into space.

Incoming energy from the Sun

CO_2 builds up in atmosphere.

Some heat escapes from the atmosphere.

Burning fossil fuels release CO_2.

Extra heat trapped by greenhouse gases causes an increase in atmospheric temperatures.

Burning coal, oil, gas, wood, and similar fuels produces carbon dioxide and other environmental pollutants.

28

Inhalers ease wheezing.

Acid rain produced by remote pollution sources seeps into rivers and lakes, kills fish, and damages trees.

GLOBAL WARMING

As carbon dioxide gas collects in the atmosphere, it likely increases the average daily temperature around the globe. This global warming may affect the world's seasonal climates, melt polar icecaps, raise sea levels, flood low-lying land, and disrupt weather patterns, farming, and wildlife. The solution: conserve energy by burning fewer fossil fuels.

ACID RAIN

Fumes from coal-fired power plants contain many chemicals. Some rise into the air and dissolve in clouds that then produce acid rain. Filters or scrubbers in chimneys and smokestacks help reduce the problem. The main solution is to conserve energy.

HOW ACID RAIN FORMS

Chemicals in the fumes from burning coal include sulphur and nitrogen oxides. These drift high in the air and dissolve in tiny water droplets in clouds, making the water acidic. The droplets merge and fall as acid rain, harming plants, animals, and the soil.

Sulphur and nitrogen from burning fossil fuels flows downwind.

Acid rain falls far away.

Wind

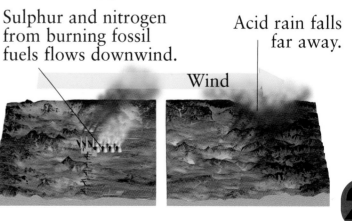

FUTURE COAL ENERGY

World coal supplies should last for another two centuries. By then, scientists and researchers should discover a cleaner, more energy-efficient alternative fuel.

CLEAN AND EFFICIENT

Coal will remain a valuable energy source for many years in the future. Methods of extracting more of coal's stored energy — such as converting coal slurry to hydrogen gas for fuel cells — will improve.

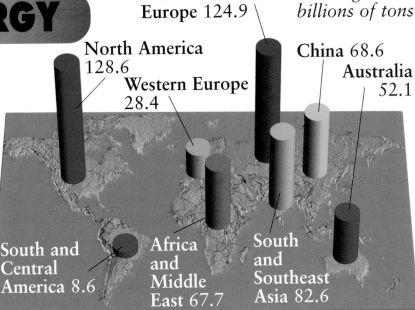

Russia and Eastern Europe 124.9

Figures in billions of tons

North America 128.6

Western Europe 28.4

China 68.6

Australia 52.1

South and Central America 8.6

Africa and Middle East 67.7

South and Southeast Asia 82.6

More than 550 billion tons of coal can be mined using present methods. Future technology should help stretch this supply.

HYDROGEN FROM COAL

Coal slurry combined with calcium oxide (lime) produces hydrogen gas and calcium carbonate (limestone). The hydrogen powers fuel cells that generate electricity. Heat helps recycle the calcium chemicals.

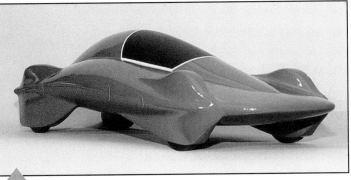

Steam-powered supercars of the future may have engines that use coal for fuel.

AFTER COAL

Coal won't last forever. Increased conservation practices and the use of fuels from renewable sources must be the goal for future energy needs.

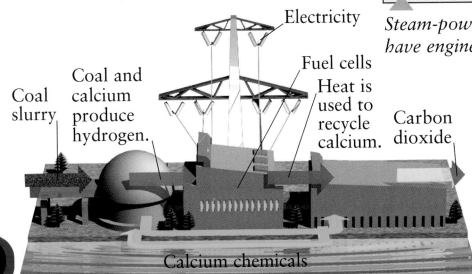

Electricity

Coal and calcium produce hydrogen.

Fuel cells

Heat is used to recycle calcium.

Carbon dioxide

Coal slurry

Calcium chemicals

combust: to combine with oxygen and burn, producing heat and light.

dissolve: to cause tiny solid particles to disperse throughout a liquid (called the solvent) and seemingly disappear.

gasify: to turn a solid substance into gases or vapors by heating.

global warming: an increase in the average annual temperature around the world, thought to be caused by trapped atmospheric pollutants.

greenhouse gases: gases or vapors in the atmosphere that prevent the Sun's heat from escaping to outer space.

overburden: soil and rock layers above a seam of coal.

renewable: reusable or recyclable.

scrubbing: the process of filtering and cleaning pollutants from fumes, smoke, and vapors emitted by industrial practices, factories, and power plants.

turbine: a type of heavy machinery with fan-like, angled blades attached to a central shaft that spins when under pressure from wind or liquids.

vapor: a gas; can be turned into a liquid (condensed) by cooling.

MORE BOOKS TO READ

Coal Power of the Future: New Ways of Turning Coal into Energy. John Riddle (Rosen)

Fossil Fuels. Energy Forever (series). Ian S. Graham (Raintree/Steck Vaughn)

Renewing Energy. Our World: Our Future (series). Sharon Dalgleish (Chelsea)

What If We Run Out of Fossil Fuels? Kimberly M. Miller (Children's Book Press)

WEB SITES

Get some fast facts about coal use in the United States. *www.nma.org/statistics/pub_fast_facts.asp*

Learn the history of fossil fuel use for energy. *www.energyquest.ca.gov/story/chapter08.html*

Due to the dynamic nature of the Internet, some web sites stay current longer than others. To find additional web sites, use a reliable search engine with one or more of the following keywords: *air pollution, coal, electric power plants, greenhouse gases, hydrogen fuel cells, mercury emissions.*

INDEX